# Responsible Tax Credits for Health Insurance

# Responsible Tax Credits for Health Insurance

Mark V. Pauly

and

John S. Hoff

The AEI Press

*Publisher for the American Enterprise Institute*

WASHINGTON, D.C.

*2002*

**Library of Congress Cataloging-in-Publication Data**

Pauly, Mark V., 1941-
    Responsible tax credits for health insurance/ Mark V. Pauly and John S. Hoff.
        p. cm.
    ISBN 0-8447-7161-9 (pbk.)
    1. Tax Credits—United States. 2. Insurance, Health—United States.
I. Hoff, John S. II. Title.
HJ4653.C73 P38 2001
336.2´06—dc21

                                                  2001046450

1 3 5 7 9 10 8 6 4 2

The AEI Press
Publisher for the American Enterprise Institute
1150 17th Street, N.W., Washington, D.C. 20036

# Contents

VI  CONTENTS

# Foreword

The possibility of passing legislation to provide health insurance coverage for all citizens has been a central issue in health policy for the past half-century. In 1965 the United States did establish public programs to expand health coverage to the aged and disabled (Medicare) and to low-income women and children (Medicaid) and did establish less extensive programs for specific populations. But the nation has chosen to rely on individuals, employers, and states to provide health insurance coverage rather than follow the example of Japan and several European countries in providing universal coverage. As a result, more than 60 percent of the population have health insurance coverage through their place of employment or other private coverage, with 25 percent covered by various government programs. Approximately 14 percent (39 million) have no coverage (Census 2001).

A relatively large proportion of the uninsured are children (22 percent are younger than eighteen) and young adults (19 percent are eighteen to twenty-four). That factor helps to explain why the issue of health insurance coverage has lasted so long as a political issue. However, a lack of political consensus to establish universal coverage is also understandable. The many reasons are both philosophic and practical. First, providing coverage requires great expense and thus meets opposition from forces concerned about adding costs to the federal budget or to employers through mandated coverage or payroll taxes. Private-sector employers—especially small businesses—that are not now required to provide health insurance have always opposed any federal or state program mandating such coverage. One study estimated that the mandates in the Clinton health plan would have added $40 billion to 1993 budget costs, would have reduced the annual earnings of previously uninsured workers by more than 7 percent, and would have reduced employment among those workers by about 800,000 (O'Neill and O'Neill 1994).

Physicians and other health-sector groups have also opposed legislation to expand coverage: some feared the expansion of federal regulation, and others did not consider proposals sufficiently comprehensive. Despite a general agreement on the imperative to reduce the number of the uninsured, the divergent objectives of the various political factions have prevented a political compromise. As one health policy analyst put it, the only thing everyone could agree on was everyone else's second choice (Altman 1999).

Has anything changed to unlock the political stalemate? Leading candidates in the 2000 presidential campaign created an ounce of political optimism with their health policy proposals. Although the proposals differed in the details, they shared a common goal of seeking to provide health insurance coverage to the uninsured. And they all used some form of tax credit as the mechanism for subsidizing the purchase of health insurance (Helms 2001). After the contentious election, interest in the use of tax credits has remained the one bipartisan element of the health policy debate. Most proposals to reduce the number of uninsured rely on a tax credit. In a perhaps surprising development, the terrorist attacks intensified interest in tax credits as a way to help the increasing number who have lost coverage because of the attacks or the slowing economy.

Still, as this study confirms, the use of tax credits encounters considerable political opposition and concern about the technical aspects. To provide a new analytical and objective assessment of the issues, the American Enterprise Institute turned to Mark V. Pauly and John S. Hoff, two of the authors of an AEI study of tax credits (Pauly, Danzon, Feldstein, and Hoff 1991, 1992). The authors chose to include the word *responsible* in their title for two reasons. First, this study can be considered an extension of their earlier study *Responsible National Health Insurance*. Second, the current study is *responsible* in the sense that it attempts to outline an approach that would promote the expansion of efficient health insurance without attempting to solve every conceivable policy or technical problem.

Their study is *responsible* in another sense, which they could not have anticipated. The authors completed their study before the terrorist attacks of September 11, 2001. While the effects of those horrific events have increased the political desire to provide immediate aid to the unemployed, they have not changed the fundamental reasons why more than 38 million American do not have health insurance coverage. As the authors show, tax credits can provide an efficient way to target federal subsidies to the uninsured poor without creating perverse incentives for individuals to overinsure or for employers to drop group coverage. Staying focused on those policy objectives remains the *responsible* way to help those newly affected by the attacks.

ROBERT B. HELMS
American Enterprise Institute

# 1

# Introduction

The 1990s saw no progress in rationalizing the financing of health care. In the early 1990s the number of the uninsured had risen, and medical care spending continued to grow at high rates. The dual trend, coupled with a political climate thought conducive to a massive new government program, tempted the Clinton administration early in the decade to offer a plan that would effectively have subjected the health care sector to substantial government regulation and control. The proposal suffered a resounding defeat, and no major reform plan has surfaced since. Unfortunately about as many people are uninsured now as when the plan was debated, and the rate of increase in health spending is again creeping upward. But fortunately the fate of the Clinton proposal and successive developments have changed the economic and political climate for reform. The table has been cleared for other approaches.

## The Voucher and Credit Approach

The approach discussed in this study is both old and new. Early in the 1990s we proposed (Pauly et al. 1991, 1992) the use of refundable tax credits or vouchers to assist and encourage people to obtain and retain insurance coverage. Under the refundable tax-credit approach, taxpayers who purchased insurance would receive a credit in a specified dollar amount, which they could apply against their federal income and payroll taxes. Reducing the tax liability would thus create funds to pay insurance premiums. If the credit were more than their total tax liability, it would be "refunded." The financial assistance would be distributed through a voucher of a specified dollar amount that could be applied toward the insurance premium.

Credits and vouchers resurfaced in specific proposals from three presidential candidates (Bill Bradley, George W. Bush, and Al Gore) in the 2000 election. The *New York Times* of September 24, 2000, added its necessary imprimatur in editorializing that a tax credit is the "straightforward way to reduce the number of uninsured Americans." President Bush

1

included a tax credit in his budget. Support is broadening for the general idea of a credit or voucher as the basis for reform—at first incremental and ultimately fundamental—in the way Americans pay for medical goods and services.

A credit/voucher is better than a tax deduction. A credit/voucher allows the subsidy to be directed to those lower-income or high-risk people who need it most, while a deduction provides more subsidy to those with higher taxable incomes. Moreover, a credit or voucher can be specified in any amount, while a deduction makes the financial assistance proportional to the person's marginal tax rate.

Some critics of our earlier proposal complained that the idea was deficient because it "boils down to little more than an adjustment of tax subsidies" and failed to regulate quality, provider payment, insurance administration, and a host of other dimensions of insurance contracts and medical services (Himmelstein and Woolhandler 1991). In contrast we believed then and think now that instead of trying to fashion a program that addresses all issues in the health care system, it is far better to begin with a simple concept that will provide a means for working out those issues. The critical first step is determining who controls the money that goes into the health care system. The entity that controls the money will ultimately determine the structure of the health care system and define its attributes.

There is a fundamental question: Will the consumer ultimately have control over the money to be spent on his health care and health insurance (even if some of it initially comes from other taxpayers through the government), or will someone else (the government or employers) have a monopoly of that power? Our past plan and our current one would assist people (in an amount determined by the democratic process) to obtain insurance and then would have policymakers stand back while consumers exercised control. Practical problems would develop soon enough, but the powerful core idea could preserve a coherence and a transparency woefully lacking in the ultracomplex Clinton plan of 1994 and in the various Medicaid-based and regulatory repairs (that is, the Health Insurance Portability and Accountability Act of 1996, or HIPAA, and state laws) that followed and are still being proposed.

The credit/voucher idea is based on the fundamental assumption that there is merit in preserving, improving, and enhancing a private, innovative, and flexible health care system; that the system depends on a private insurance system to provide financing; and that as many people as possible should be able to participate in it. Without a system of private insurance, only government can spread risk and pay claims. Such a situation inevitably would bring government control over the health care system, as Medicare is increasingly demonstrating. Thus the more people who can participate in a private insurance market, the greater the number who can benefit from free choice and the more secure a private health care system can be.

Many people are uninsured because the costs of care and thus the market price of insurance are too high relative to their willingness or ability to pay. Credits would reduce that price by offering individuals earmarked purchasing power; the reduced price would stimulate voluntary efforts to obtain insurance coverage. If the credits were sufficiently large, if they were designed to be financially neutral across a variety of competitive plans, and if most buyers were reasonably well informed, the resulting choices should lead to two mutually reinforcing benefits: increases in the proportion of the population with insurance and, for the insured, the attainment of levels of quality, price, and rates of adoption of new technology that represent a proper balancing of costs and benefits. Credits offer the prospect of adequate access to insurance and care that consumers desire (regardless of what medical administrators, working for government or employers, may prefer). And that prospect is the main social objective of health care financing policy.

## The Purpose of This Study

The authors of this study participated on a team that prepared one of the first refundable tax-credit proposals more than a decade ago (Pauly et al. 1991). The first Bush administration, in its proposal for credits for the uninsured, included many aspects of the original analysis. However, political opposition in Congress, the proposal's unnecessarily complex form, and budget issues stymied such change. The continued interest in refundable tax credits for the uninsured makes it useful to revisit the key questions about the rationale for credits and to discuss the elements that any credit plan ought to have.

In this study we begin by reviewing the changes in the economic and political environment that have provided a new stage on which to place credits. We next suggest how credits might function and how a credit plan should be tailored to the new economic and political circumstances. We show that inevitable trade-offs in credit design require social and political discussion. We outline important features for a credit plan that fits the new situation and conclude with a description of a sample plan and a discussion of its administrative and political feasibility.

# 2

# Changes in Attitudes about Health Issues

### New Realism

The failure of the Clinton approach and the increased realism that resulted have made practical reform possible now. The failure of the Clinton proposal—in part because of its complexity and sweeping scope—reminds us that grand schemes are not in the cards. Health policy, like other issues in American society, will proceed gradually.

The focus must instead be on interim steps. Rather than make illusory promises for all, reform proposals must demonstrate modest—and realistic—improvements in the right direction. Immediate perfection is impossible, but substantial improvements are not.

In the mid-1990s the private sector was able to rein in cost increases relative to the much higher trend of the previous thirty-five years. We now know that private insurance can live within financial constraints if necessary. In more recent years, when greater prosperity was achieved with a flourish, people decided to spend more of their new income on costly medical technology and to get out from under the more burdensome cost-containment measures of health maintenance organizations. The key point is the knowledge that we have choices; there is no cost-increasing imperative. The rate of growth in spending is a choice—one subject to real trade-offs, but a choice nonetheless. Limits on financial resources and political reality mean that reform will be measured, not massive, and incremental and thoughtful, not comprehensive and forced. The public understands therefore that the presumed perfect should no longer be the mortal enemy of the moderately good. That recognition increases the attractiveness of realistic measures to deal with the persistently high numbers of the uninsured without imposing a massive government program and without rekindling unchecked growth in spending.

Though salutary (and perhaps obvious in hindsight), the lesson raises a new question at the heart of the debate on covering the uninsured.

4

For political and economic reasons, and for the preservation of a private health care system, we are not about to launch a massive national health insurance program in which the government finances most care for most Americans (or all for all, as the advocates of "universal" coverage would have it). We must therefore decide the categories of citizens and the types of expenses on which to focus. If the government does not finance all care for all Americans, we need to set priorities to determine whom it assists in the private insurance market. To do so, we need to value or weight various deviations from the supposed ideal of universality and judge which imperfections would be most tolerable and which improvements would do the most good. The process is basic and unavoidable, though rarely mentioned, and the choices are difficult because the best option is far from obvious.

Specifically, for any given amount of money in the government budget earmarked for assisting people to obtain coverage, the government could take different tacks with different results. The amount of the credit and how it was structured would affect which categories of people bought more insurance. The government could attempt to ensure that some higher-risk Americans purchase insurance (at higher cost). As the government spent more money to assist higher-risk people, less money would be available to assist others. Conversely the government could encourage a larger number of Americans at lower average risk (children, young women, and young men) to obtain generous coverage. Or the funding could cause almost all uninsured to obtain some, though limited, coverage.

If the most comprehensive coverage for everybody is not now an option—and realists know that it is not—which of the three strategies would be most desirable? That question can be answered only if we have some basis for assessing the value of coverage for some high-risk Americans against coverage for a larger number of low risks and for weighing a few extra dollars of coverage for those who already have some coverage against catastrophic coverage for those who otherwise would have no coverage at all.

And the calculus is not simply one of dividing up valuable tax funds according to the judgments about desired changes in peoples' coverage. In providing subsidies for the purchase of insurance, we must make judgments on what is fair—not only among those who do not have insurance but also with respect to those who obtain insurance but receive relatively small subsidies or none at all. Should citizens who obtained their own insurance be treated differently and denied the same assistance given to others who were similarly situated in all other respects?

No technical measure can determine the ideal balance. The valuation and the allocation of benefits are political questions. Raising the issue begins the search for options that might inform the political debate. We outline a variety of approaches that span a set of policy choices. The public and its representatives can use these examples to judge what they prefer. In that way they can elicit the values implicitly placed on different configurations and can reach solutions most closely approaching what the American public wants.

### New Alliances

Surprisingly broad bipartisan political agreement supports the use of credits. In 2000 the presidential candidates of both major parties embraced the idea—at least to some extent. Members of Congress, especially in the House of Representatives, have also expressed support and designed specific plans that would use credits. Given a history of failed political initiatives to deal with the uninsured, nothing guarantees that at long last vote-seekers are willing to defer their own ideal plan for one that would merely do some good. But as a *New York Times* editorial endorsing tax credits demonstrates, a better chance now exists for putting this approach into effect than for any other approach for a long time.

### Less Concern over Cost

Public attitudes on health care issues have seen another major change: a lessening of concern about rising costs—at least for now. Ironically, as the rate of growth in spending tailed off, higher medical spending developed an improved reputation.

For several important categories of illness (principally heart disease and stroke), health indicators have improved rapidly, and more evidence indicates that higher medical spending has been at least partly responsible (Cutler, McClellan, and Newhouse 1998; Triplett 1999). Such improvement in the quality of care—not merely the inputs but, more important, the outcomes—has become so pronounced and so obvious that many scholars have urged that the medical care price index take into account quality improvements and that it be ignored until those corrections are made (Pauly 1999a).

In addition, the source of spending growth has shifted from an increase in unit prices for hospital episodes and doctor visits in the 1980s to an increase in the kind, quality, and quantity of prescription drugs and devices in the 1990s. We now think that we get something of real value for our extra money.

For example, the amount spent on drugs is increasing more rapidly than spending on other components of medical services because of the success of new pharmaceutical products. The increase in spending results much more from increased use—the availability of new products or use of older products in new ways—than from increased prices (Berndt 2000; Calfee 2000). Nevertheless some political efforts are being made to impose price controls on drugs (directly or by attempting to import foreign price-control mechanisms). Although price increases have not contributed greatly to the recent growth in spending on drugs (compared with increases in the use of drugs), price controls proposed by some policy-makers would reduce companies' incentives to engage in long-range and risky research to develop new drugs. The profit margins of drug companies are not sacred; the current flow of new products is not necessarily at the optimal level. However, cost containment through government-determined price controls would inevitably and unavoidably impose a cost in terms of fewer beneficial new products.

Despite the danger in speculating on how data will be interpreted, the slowdown in spending growth and the increase in the perceived value of the purchases have probably eased the pressure for controlling spending. People are coming to appreciate—as we argued in our earlier analysis against the then-prevailing wisdom—that higher spending on medical care is not harmful per se and that the appropriate response to increases in spending depends on the value of the funded objects over the value of other uses. The willingness to pay higher amounts even for improved products is not unlimited, but it surely exists and is manifested in behavior. Enthusiasm has ebbed for types of health coverage, such as restrictive HMOs, whose singular virtue in practical application proved to be an ability to reduce costs. The earlier enthusiasm has actually turned into a backlash, now particularly evident in legislation for a so-called patients' bill of rights.

The survey evidence on that matter is of limited value because it usually asks simple questions—Do you want lower costs?—and does not induce respondents to look at trade-offs. The evidence does strongly suggest that when people are given a serious price tag for some benefit (such as the right to sue), their support drops. The proportion believing that medical costs, while high, are still reasonable rose between 1973 and 1996 (Bowman 1998). But the strongest evidence is obtained, not from surveys, but from behavior. Even as spending growth increased after 1997, at least in a period of prosperity employees were not asking for their health benefits to be cut so that they could have larger monetary raises.

### Demand for More Choice

It has been evident to employers, politicians, and analysts that as middle-class Americans have realized that the amount spent for their health care can be too low and too constraining, they have sought more control over what they get and how they get it. Two developments in particular have resulted. Enthusiasm for more permissive health plans, even if at modestly higher premiums, is much higher than ten years ago—perhaps because of labor shortages and the high level at which the general economy has recently operated. And perhaps more important, people appreciate more the value of choice across health plans as well as choice among providers and medical products. As plans have become restrictive, people have come to recognize that plan choice largely determines provider choices.

# 3

# Changes in the Economic Environment for Health Care

We have discussed changes in attitudes about the health care sector. Now we discuss changes in its actual performance.

## New Success in Cost Containment

The most striking change in the environment of health economics is the fact that both the private and public sectors have found ways to hold down the rate of growth of spending.

The private sector was there first. Beginning in 1994, it exhibited real growth rates much lower than the 5–7 percent that had characterized medical spending since 1965. Most surprisingly the private sector was able to hold down growth not just for a year or two, but for five years. Real private-sector growth in spending per insured person was virtually zero in some years. Although reliable data for 2000 are not yet in, they will probably show somewhat higher real rates of growth in spending, though still well below the growth rates of the previous three decades.

The government took longer to get its cost-containment act together, perhaps because the relaxation of limits on home health care benefits and other legislated adjustments bumped up Medicare spending in the mid-1990s. But by 1997 aggregate spending growth in both Medicare and Medicaid was under better control, and in 1998 and 1999 Medicare out-did the private sector in achieving almost no growth in nominal terms and negative growth in real terms.

Significantly Medicare contained its costs relative to private insurance in part because it did not cover the fastest-growing cost item, outpatient prescription drugs, although its beneficiaries do have to pay for such drugs. Also significantly Medicare achieved low spending growth not by reducing the use of care, but by reducing what it pays hospitals, doctors, home health agencies, and HMOs to meet budget targets—despite the threat to access and quality that such reductions represent. The program

9

used its regulatory authority to force down reimbursements even if beneficiaries might have paid more to secure better access and quality.

The primary conclusion is that public and private spending growth, far from being inexorable or inevitable, can be modified or *chosen* in both private and political contexts by people who feel a strong enough need to do so. The finding does not tell us what we should or will choose, but the newfound sense of power over the environment makes it more plausible to assume that a program to cover the uninsured can be managed and controlled. Growth will be affected by new technology, but it is also affected by demand and values, not only for health care but also for what must be sacrificed to pay for it. We have greater confidence that the public can choose the desired rate of growth. People may choose moderately high levels, but regardless of the choice, a foreboding sense of unavoidable financial doom need no longer block our desire and will to provide coverage for the uninsured.

### The Federal Budget

In the budget-constrained environment of the 1990s, we felt it necessary to show where the money would come from to pay for credits for the uninsured. To raise money and to implement good policy, we proposed recycling the $125 billion-plus annual tax subsidy for health insurance purchased by the employer on behalf of the distinctly non–low-income employee. The change would still be good tax policy; it would remove distorted incentives to purchase too much insurance and to rely on the employer to arrange it rather than to purchase it individually.

It is still highly desirable to reform the tax treatment of employer-paid health insurance, but it is now possible to move ahead on credits for the uninsured without waiting for that tax change. The uninsured can be covered without raising taxes on those who have employer-provided insurance if Congress is willing to step up to the plate and provide a modest amount of funding for a modest tax credit along the responsible lines that we are suggesting. If we target tax cuts, using them to help low-income people afford the purchase of insurance is an attractive target.

### Changes in Purchasing Insurance

**Employment-Based Insurance.** Mutually reinforcing changes in expert opinion on the purchasing and preferred types of health insurance have also changed the economic environment of health care. Around 1990, most experts spoke with a near-uniform voice: employers should buy their employees managed-care insurance, and employers should—and indeed were best qualified to—decide the best plan. But now the assumption that the employer should determine an individual's health care plan and the notion that conventional managed care is the appropriate choice are receiving increasing re-examination. The HMO backlash may well have been carried too far, but two facts have become crystal clear: whatever merits managed-care plans have, they are not for everyone and the people who are subject to the restrictions imposed by managed care should receive the benefit of the savings in an explicit and clear fashion. The limits of the employment-based system in reaching most of the uninsured, even the employed uninsured, are becoming increasingly evident.

We have discussed the drawbacks of selective subsidies of employment-based insurance elsewhere (Pauly 1992, 1994a, 1994b; Pauly, Percy, and Herring 1999b). Such a policy is opaque and restricted, distorted and unfair. Most experts now understand that Americans—particularly those who cannot use employment-based insurance (Arnett 1999)—should be offered other ways for arranging coverage.

**Alternatives.** The last change is easily overlooked because it occurs in only a limited part of the system. But that part is potentially important, with a capacity for improvement and expansion. The individual insurance market, small and imperfect as it is, already is looking better and performing better than in the past. Not only has nongroup insurance improved in many dimensions; recent research shows that employment-based group insurance is not uniquely good at one of the main functions for which it is praised: it does not pool risk, even within the group, much more effectively than nongroup insurance does (Pauly and Herring 1999). While employee-paid premium shares are usually uniform, the reduction in older workers' wages to cover the employee-paid share appears larger than that of younger workers' wages.

That change in purchasing health insurance suggests that a significant proportion of Americans can obtain their health insurance as they buy other insurance and other goods and services—in competitive private markets in which individuals choose for themselves. Flexibility in transferring earmarked purchasing power to individuals—through employers' defined contribution programs and government tax credits or vouchers—enhanced by electronic methods to sell and administer health insurance could give employees and all other Americans workable alternatives to employer management of their health insurance.

## Political Changes

Independent of individual preferences and attitudes, the operation of politics is changing. The old favorites of reform will not work. Government policies requiring that any major segment of the population obtain insurance without a subsidy now seem to be considered both undesirable and politically unacceptable. Even mandates that require people to take subsidized insurance are widely suspect. Such a negative reaction probably resulted from the poorly designed mandate in the Clinton plan; in one of its longest-lasting effects, that debacle discredited any form of mandate, even with subsidies. Greater concern revolves around the efficacy and the fairness of government-imposed requirements and their effect on personal freedom.

The notion that the regulation of insurance coverage and premium setting can seriously address the problem of the uninsured has also proved unacceptable: mandated benefit packages would drive lower-income consumers away, and community rating (without mandated purchase) drives low risks away. At best the effect of community rating on the number of the uninsured (without a politically infeasible mandate) would be a wash. At the same time it would present a real risk that insurers would pull out and thereby worsen the problem. Efforts in both Kentucky and Washington have shown the limits of regulation in compelling sellers (or more accurately buyers) of private insurance to subsidize or cross-subsidize coverage. The patients' bill of rights, though purporting to benefit those who have insurance, may well raise premiums more than its value and could increase the number of uninsured.

# 4

# Design Issues

## Target Populations

The first question that must be addressed is how the credit/voucher should be targeted. A credit plan must fit with the existing system of subsidies for low-income Americans. Medicaid subsidizes care for some low-income people under state eligibility and benefit rules with federal regulation. Other low-income people receive "free" care—care that is paid for by charities, by non-Medicaid government subsidies, by the providers who give the care, and by the insured who use those providers. But another, larger subsidy is inversely related to poverty. The exclusion of employer-paid insurance premiums from employees' taxable income substantially lowers taxes on total compensation, primarily for non–low-income workers.

The voucher/credit should be available to all those who would otherwise receive Medicaid or a significant amount of free care. State regulations complicate Medicaid, with eligibility limited to the low-income of certain ages, sexes, and family arrangements. Reliance on charity care may cause individuals to forgo needed treatment at earlier stages of disease. Both subsidy systems may make the recipient feel stigmatized.

Those otherwise eligible for Medicaid should be eligible for the credit/voucher; thus they would have an alternative to the current monopoly Medicaid program. Those not eligible for Medicaid who now fall back on free care, out of choice or ignorance, also should have the opportunity for an insurance voucher. But opportunities for choice must persist. Providing a voucher to cover the full cost of policies with adequate coverage similar to those bought by their fellow-citizens would relieve low-income individuals of stigma, give them the same choice among plans and providers that better-off people regard as valuable, and increase the opportunity for responsibility.

Charity could still provide care not covered by public insurance (just as it can supplement Medicaid now). A fallback public insurance option

13

(either the Medicaid package or some other) should be available on neutral terms to those who did not choose to take private insurance, including those not eligible for Medicaid. State governments could be authorized to use the value of the credit on behalf of individuals to place them in insurance programs if they did not choose insurance on their own.

The current economy would allow funding for low-income people if voters chose to do so. With careful measurement of income and with a sensible phase-out of subsidies, extending fully subsidized private coverage to low-income people not covered by Medicaid—principally able-bodied men and women without children—would not harm economywide incentives. Giving people now covered by Medicaid a choice to spend the same amount on alternatives to the public plan would not raise the government's cost but would give the low-income access to private insurance on a predictable basis and would remove them from the episodic eligibility of Medicaid.

For people at somewhat higher income levels above Medicaid eligibility, more variation in coverage and subsidy would be possible, but more complex design issues would arise. The primary issues would concern those with incomes high enough that they could pay part of, but not the entire, premium for what society considered adequate insurance coverage. More than half the people with income levels of 100–200 percent of the poverty line have already arranged for at least some private insurance, primarily by choosing jobs that pay part of their compensation in the form of insurance premiums, even with low tax subsidies. Most people in those groups are willing to make sacrifices for health insurance, but all of them need help, especially if the goal is the fair financing of reasonably generous coverage.

The uninsured need help in buying coverage; the insured deserve equal assistance. The group of non–low-income, non–high-income is the main target for insurance credits or vouchers. Table 1 shows that the group, defined as those with family incomes between 125 percent and 300 percent of the poverty line, made up nearly 40 percent of the uninsured and significantly outnumbered the uninsured in poverty.

As table 1 indicates, the 40 percent of the uninsured fall in the range of 125–300 percent of the federal poverty line (FPL), a larger percentage than those less than 125 percent (about a third) or those greater than 300 percent (nearly 30 percent). Uninsured people are in families at all income levels, but unsurprisingly the most "typical" uninsured person is in a lower-middle-income family.

**TABLE 1**

THOSE WITHOUT HEALTH INSURANCE, AT AGES 0–64,
BY INCOME AS PERCENTAGE OF FEDERAL POVERTY LINE, 1999
(N=115,474)

| Family Income (% of poverty line) | Percent of the Uninsured | |
|---|---|---|
| Less than 100 | 25.1 | } 32.6 |
| 100–124 | 7.5 | |
| 125–149 | 8.1 | |
| 150–174 | 7.5 | |
| 175–199 | 6.0 | } 39.9 |
| 200–249 | 10.4 | |
| 250–299 | 7.9 | |
| 300–399 | 10.0 | |
| 400–499 | 6.5 | } 27.6 |
| 500 and more | 11.1 | |
| Total | 100 | |

NOTE: The table uses post-1996 CPS health insurance variables and appropriate CPS March Supplement weights to reflect national population. Data set is CPS March Supplement for 2000 and reflects coverage in 1999.

At some point, as discussed later, the subsidy would phase out for higher-income individuals. We assume that (contrary to our recommendations in 1992) as a matter of political reality, the subsidy provided through the exclusion for employer-provided insurance would continue for the present.

### Preliminaries

Virtually all policy issues entail trade-offs. The most obvious trade-off in tax credits for health insurance balances relatively easy administration with the precise targeting of the subsidy. Should a given subsidy be available to a wide range of people for a wide variety of plans, or should a precisely specified plan have a specific subsidy?

Simplicity of administration minimizes costs and increases public acceptance. A program that gave the same credit or voucher to every person would be easily administered. But the program would have an obvious drawback. The use of tax money to provide large credits to rich women or healthy employed young men might be questioned. The most perfectly targeted plan for tax credits would be complex. Opting for simplicity would mean tolerating some imperfections.

The more credits reflect individual circumstances or characteristics, the greater the incentive might be for an individual to change his behavior to obtain the maximum credit. Suppose that we offered generous credits to people who accepted jobs that did not pay part of their compensation as insurance premiums, but we did not offer them to similarly situated and equally skilled people with employer-paid coverage. We would be providing an incentive for people to select jobs that do not carry health insurance.

The technical term for what we seek here is *incentive neutrality*: other things equal, we prefer a system of credits or vouchers that distorts individual behavior not related to health insurance as little as possible. But neutral incentives often increase budgetary expenditures (but not real resource costs).

We also need to find some way of dealing with variation in risk, especially a large (relative to a person's income) and unpredictable variation, such as the onset of a high-cost chronic condition. Some methods of designing and marketing insurance—in particular, guaranteed renewability—could substantially reduce the extent to which people faced unexpected variations in premiums when their own risk changed. Other variations would need either some adjustment to credits, some complementary mechanism (for example, a high-risk pool financed from general revenues), or some combination of the two.

Thus the competing goals of ease of administration, neutral incentives, efficiency, equity, and public budget responsibility present a Rubik's cube of health policy. Compromise and trade-offs are inevitable. Quantifying or valuing the trade-offs is often difficult, and different groups view them differently. No matter what balance is struck, some people on the margin will be pushed in one direction or another by a fiscal feather.

## A Possible Structure

Judging the impact of any credit proposal on insurance purchasing and on equity entails three basic questions: (1) What set of premiums would individuals using the credit face when they shopped for insurance? (2) What amount would the consumer be willing to pay in addition to the credit for each possible insurance option? (3) How much should people have left to spend on other things after they paid what we have asked for insurance?

The answer to the first question turns on the market in which insurance is sold. The answer to the second question depends on the money value that an individual attaches to different insurances—what economists call the *reservation price* for insurance. The third question depends on what we mean by *fairness*.

Broadly speaking, a credit or a voucher would be used in two types of markets. One would be the *individual market* for health insurance. The other would be some type of *group market*, including alternatives to the employment-based group. We describe how various credit systems might work in helping people buy insurance in either the individual market or in a new type of group market where an individual explicitly pays the premium.

A credit scheme must specify two things: (1) the characteristics of policies that qualify for the credit and (2) the determinants of the dollar value of the credit. For example, one simple, though restrictive, version of such a scheme would provide an adult with a credit worth $1,000 toward the premium of an insurance policy providing certain specified levels of coverage for different medical services. An individual would not keep the unused portion of the credit if he found a policy that met the requirements with a premium less than $1,000 but would be required to pay any additional premium for a qualified policy that cost more than $1,000.

Determining whether a person would buy insurance under that scenario would depend on the existence of a qualified policy with a premium $Pr$ that satisfied $(Pr-1{,}000) < RP$, where $RP$ was a person's reservation price for the specified policy. That is, a person would buy insurance if some qualified policy on the market cost less above the amount of the credit than the value placed on the insurance policy. The amount of the credit would thus be a critical design element with a substantial effect on how frequently credits were used to buy insurance. The other critical dimension would be how the coverage qualifications were translated into premiums in the insurance market. Regulations requiring more coverage in the qualified plan generally translate into higher premiums. Even with a subsidy, requiring "better" coverage might reduce the number of people willing to pay extra to get it.

The higher the maximum dollar value of the credit and the less restrictive the rules on its end-use, the greater the number of people who would use the credit. A given dollar credit at any level would more likely be used by people charged lower premiums for a specified policy— people who presented lower risk, lived in lower-cost geographic areas, or were more efficient, more eager, or luckier in finding lower-priced insurance.

The credit, however, need not have a flat dollar value. Instead it could be defined in terms of a proportion of the premium paid by the individual. Suppose the credit is $P$ percent of the premium for the person of average risk who lives in the average-cost area and suppose such a percentage credit amounts to $X on average. Compared with the fixed-dollar credit paying also $X, a scheme covering P percent would pay less than $X in absolute terms for those paying premiums below the average and more than $X for those paying above the average. Higher premiums would probably be charged to people who commanded higher average benefits, including both higher health risks and some average risks who obtain more costly care. Compared with an "equivalent" fixed-dollar credit, a proportional credit automatically would give a higher dollar subsidy to higher risks, those living in higher-cost areas, those choosing more comprehensive coverage, and those making less effort to find policies with low premiums. Even with a proportional credit, those who faced a higher premium (for any reason) would still pay more in absolute terms.

Compared with uniform dollar credits, proportional credits combine partial risk adjustment (often desirable) with incentives for average risks to overpurchase insurance (less desirable). That is, because the size of the subsidy that proportional credits provided would vary directly with the premium, the credits would also subsidize normal risks who chose to buy lavish coverage.

A credit could combine the proportional and fixed-dollar features. The credit might be P percent of the premium's cost up to a maximum credit cap of Z dollars (equivalent to a premium of Z/P dollars). (If $P = 0.9$ and $Z = 1,000$, for example, the buyer would pay the full cost of any additional premium in excess of $1,111 = 1,000/0.9.)

The acceptance rate of a credit would depend on its administration as well as on its value. Take the least restrictive specification of an eligible policy as an example. Suppose that a person were offered a flat (not proportional) health insurance credit of $1,000 that was good for any qualified policy. He would have no reason to buy a policy with a premium less than the credit—doing so would waste some of the credit. An insurance policy would qualify for the credit if state insurance regulators had approved it for sale in the state.

If the credit were easy to claim, and eligible people were properly informed, nearly 100 percent of those eligible for such a credit would probably claim it. They could find a policy that could be purchased for the amount of the credit; they would be offered a fully subsidized or free insurance policy. Those who did not apply for coverage could automatically be assigned to a plan. Some people (probably those with lower income or risk) might choose a policy with a premium just equal to the credit, while others might spend their own money to buy a somewhat more generous policy. But everyone would be motivated to buy something. Only people who disliked insurance (or government hand-outs) would reject the credit and remain wholly uninsured.

If the process of applying for or using the credit were complex, those who did not attach as much value to the minimum policy eligible for the credit as they did to avoiding the hassle or embarrassment cost of apply-ing for a credit might not bother to apply. Such motivation presumably explains in part why about a third of the people eligible for free Medicaid for themselves or their children fail to become covered. If no one in the family were sick at the moment and if becoming eligible were a time-consuming hassle, the bother to apply might not seem rational—until insurance was needed. If a plan required people to pay the premium before receiving the credit, or required them to pay an additional amount, those with cash flow problems might decline the subsidy.

If the government could identify most people who were eligible (for example, if eligibility were fully specified by an individual's income tax status, including income low enough that no income tax was owed or no tax return form was required), they could automatically be covered by a zero net premium policy. The government could identify workers who paid payroll or income taxes, but those who owed no federal taxes of any type would have to be identified in some other way. Beyond that level the extent of information provided about the program and the form in which information was provided could be important.

Our 1992 proposal suggested a fixed-dollar credit, adjusted for income (more generous for lower-income people) and to some extent for risk, which could be applied to a specified policy. Although the amount that an individual would have to pay at any income and risk level was supposed to be appropriate and fair, a mandate would be needed to induce literally everyone to use the credit because some people might not be willing to pay the amount voluntarily that society thought they should. Other proposals with which we have considerable sympathy used pro-portional credits plus a mandate but no risk adjustment (Butler and Haislmaier 1992).

We will discuss the issues of risk adjustment below, but the present concern is how the plans would work should there be no mandate. What design features are important to get people to take coverage voluntarily? The preceding discussion suggested some key trade-offs. If—as we assume is the case—we are not going to impose a mandate, we are going to have to be less aggressive in specifying the minimum coverage, more flexible in calculating the credit, and more aggressive in marketing the credits and the insurance itself. If we limit ourselves to pushing with a string, we will have to be creative. We offer some ideas on how to do those things below.

# 5

# Two Different Groups
# for the Credit

People in two different categories would use a credit. Those in the first group do not have insurance because they will not or cannot pay the full premium charged by the insurer. They would be able and willing to pay the portion of the premium remaining after the application of the credit. They would buy the qualified insurance. The reservation price of this group for all insurance policies available to them would be less than the premiums for those policies, but their reservation price for some qualified policy would be greater than its net premium—its premium reduced by the amount of the credit.

People in the second group had already purchased insurance. They would also use the credit unless they had qualms about accepting government subsidies or were unwilling to buy a policy that was required by the terms of the credit (either because of its cost or because of the conditions that it imposed).

Evaluation of a given credit program must involve both categories of recipients. The social value of uninsured people becoming insured might appear positive. But why? And why do we care about the low-income uninsured? Answering that question is important in considering the relative value of different credit approaches. And is there any value in providing a credit to those who would have been insured anyway?

## Value of Credit for the Uninsured

The uninsured present a policy problem for three reasons. Most obvious, insurance could reduce the financial barriers that they face in receiving effective care. A data-oriented person might say that one should judge the value of covering people by the impact on their health status. Most would be willing to settle for evidence that many (if not all) would be more likely to use effective health care if they had insurance.

The second reason is that we should avoid situations in which people do pay for effective medical care but without insurance have inadequate remaining income for other values. The third reason applies even if people without insurance do receive care through charity or by a bad debt for the provider. Care obtained by the uninsured under these circumstances is likely to be more episodic and of lower quality (through no fault of the provider) than care chosen by the insured. Also, financing care for the uninsured through a bad debt or charity distributes the costs arbitrarily among certain providers, insurance plans, and insured people rather than transparently, broadly, and fairly through explicit government subsidies financed by taxes that are as fair and efficient as possible.

The availability of "free" care and a lack of familiarity with insurance might inhibit some low-income people from using the voucher credit. But many would take advantage of it. Others would grow in responsibility because they have a choice.

### Value of Credit for the Insured

What about the use of the credit by people who would purchase (in many cases have purchased) adequate insurance without a credit? Would public money spent on them be wasted? In a true economic sense the answer would unequivocally be no. The payments for their credits would represent only transfers to them and would not be associated with new uses of real resources. Providing them with credits would bear no cost of additional resource use.

For that group, a tax credit would be the equivalent of a tax cut, pure and simple, which it would surely deserve as much as the formerly uninsured who were otherwise similarly situated. Providing credits to relatively low-income people with insurance would be a matter of basic fairness, an encouragement of responsible behavior, and tax equity.

Consider two low-income households whose working members have the same skills and productivity. One chooses a job that pays only cash compensation; the other chooses a job that pays lower money wages but also pays part of the compensation in the form of insurance premiums. Shouldn't we value the more responsible behavior of the second family and reward it with the same subsidy that we used to change the behavior of the first family? (The credit for the second family should be adjusted to reflect the small subsidy for employer-paid insurance from the tax exclusion.) Both were deserving of help, but neither more obviously than the other. And principles of equity would require us to treat them identically. The equity case would be even stronger for people who bought insurance in the individual market and therefore received no tax breaks. The real issue is equal treatment; "bang for the buck" scoring by itself (cf. Gruber and Levitt 2000) is inappropriate.

In that sense one can view a tax credit as a tax cut, but one made available only to people who engaged in responsible insurance-purchasing behavior. Those in this nonpoor, nonrich population who could afford coverage (or could have taken a job that carried coverage) but chose not to do so were no more deserving of a tax cut than those who had paid careful attention and made sacrifices for coverage. It seems only fair to reward those who were responsible even before the advent of meaningful tax credits with at least as much of a financial transfer as is given to those who needed a push.

# 6

# Policy Trade-Offs

## A Simplified and Adaptive Tax-Credit Plan

Providing subsidies would assist some of the formerly uninsured in becoming insured, but how many would make the transition is uncertain. With the current generous tax exclusion, almost all of the well-off obtain insurance, although they might do so as well without large subsidies. Unfortunately the effect of moderately generous tax credits on insurance purchasing by the lower-income uninsured is unknown. Finally, the presence of the tax exclusion complicates the development of any credit scheme economically, politically, and technically. As the exclusion will not be abolished at the outset (although it could be modified), any plan must fit around it, at least at first.

Accordingly, we propose a credit scheme explicitly designed to be adaptive—exactly the right goal when policy outcomes are uncertain. We propose to begin with a plan that would make serious inroads into the problem of the uninsured and to build into the plan the capacity for change and the momentum to seek continual improvement. Building in adaptability also contributes to simplicity: if a plan is cast in concrete, it must deal with any possible contingency, whereas an adaptive plan can start simple and then change in measured ways in response to experience. By responding to specific issues that actually arise rather than trying to anticipate every problem, a program can maintain its relative simplicity and at the same time be more effective.

## The Simplest Program

The simplest credit program would offer the same fixed-dollar credit for every family unit upon the purchase of a qualified plan. As an analytical benchmark, the current employment-based tax exclusion provides an average subsidy of about $1,500 per worker. A simple credit program could offer a similar subsidy, or $1,500 per working adult. (We later argue for a different program with different credit levels, but this example is intended to serve as a benchmark.) Each individual who bought qualified health insurance using the credit could then have the premium reduced by $1,500 (thus to zero if the premium were less than $1,500). This approach raises several design issues.

### Fitted with Exclusion

The continuing existence of the tax exclusion for employer-paid insurance premiums substantially complicates even such a simple program. We do not propose to abolish that subsidy in our proposed transitional approach. However, a person who obtains insurance through a job that pays part of its compensation in the form of tax-shielded insurance premiums cannot be allowed to claim the credit and continue to exclude the employer's payment from income and payroll taxes for the same premium payment.

Instead our goal is to net out any current subsidies from a credit that the worker may claim. The simplest way to do so and to prevent such double subsidization would be to require anyone claiming the credit to report the value of employer-paid health insurance premiums as part of total taxable wages and thus forgo the benefits of the exclusion (Pauly and Goodman 1995). An alternative would be a credit equal to the difference between the gross credit amount and the value of the exclusion (if less). (The latter approach would be the equivalent of providing a person with the net gain in after-tax income that would have been obtained by surrendering the exclusion and receiving the credit but may be easier to explain and administer.) There would be no credit if the value of the exclusion were higher than the credit. A recent proposal of the Progressive Policy Institute includes a simplified version of that idea (Lemieux, Kendall, and Levine 2000). It sets a uniform credit for people who obtain employer-paid insurance that would roughly equal the difference between the credit for individual coverage and the average value of the exclusion. Thus the proposal would provide an overall subsidy to people who obtained employer-paid insurance that would roughly equal the subsidy paid to everyone else.

The processes just outlined would be both simpler to administer and less distortive than the provision in some tax-credit plans that would deny the credit altogether to workers who received or were eligible for employment-based group insurance (even if the employee paid much of the premium). Such a provision would deprive those workers of the help available through the credit. More important, it would also prevent lower-income employees from using a credit to obtain their insurance through a job-related group, even if that mechanism were the most efficient one. Either the provision is based on the fallacy that employers give insurance benefits and would keep doing so even if a credit were available, or it is an attempt to hold down budget impacts by putting obstacles in the way of access to the credit subsidy by those who deserve it.

If workers must make an either-or choice between the credit and the exclusion, we would expect workers to compare the tax advantage of the credit with that provided by the exclusion. If high-income workers shielded $4,000 of premiums from taxable income and had a combined marginal tax rate of 50 percent, they would probably be better off by declining the government's new offer of a $1,500 credit. Lower-income workers, however, would choose the credit because they would pay (low) taxes on the so-called employer contribution now treated as wage income.

### Adjusted for Income

Rather than offering the same credit to all, it would probably be preferable to vary the credit inversely with income and directly with other indicators of need to offer stronger purchase incentives to lower-income households. To encourage lower-income, lower–tax rate people to obtain insurance by using the credit, the gain from choosing the credit should be large enough to make the changes worthwhile, but the credit could be smaller (even zero) for those with high incomes and high existing tax subsidies. Our initial proposal suggested such a progressive credit structure; it is virtually a sine qua non of meaningful credit plans. If the purpose of the credit is to assist Americans to buy insurance, those who need the most help should get the largest subsidy. The credit should be refundable; it should make positive payments to those whose tax liability was less than the amount of the credit. Then it would benefit even those who paid no income taxes and whose payroll tax liability was less than the amount of the credit.

Toward the other end of the income spectrum, the credit could phase down as income increased and phase out at some income level. If the exclusion did not exist, phasing the credit down to zero would be reasonable. If the exclusion were preserved, however, equity might suggest that the credit should be equal to the average value of the exclusion at a given income level. For example, the average value of the exclusion for a single person earning $50,000 per year would be about $800 (assuming a tax-shielded employer premium contribution of $1,800, a payroll tax of 15 percent, and a marginal income tax bracket of 28 percent). Beginning with a $1,500 credit, one might phase it down to a value of $800 for persons with incomes of $50,000. At higher income levels the credit could be reduced further, but it might not be necessary to do so. Few of those receiving employment-based coverage would find it worthwhile to claim the reduced credit. It would appeal only to the small minority (at that income level) who did not obtain employer-provided insurance.

Above some high-income level, even though the continuation of the exclusion would be inequitable, there would be no need to help a person afford insurance, no need to use taxpayer funds that might be drawn from lower-income workers to provide a subsidy, and no need for the government to insert itself into what should—and in this circumstance could—be a private transaction. The well-off would need no help, and they could be left alone. In contrast, large credits for the lower-income would equip them with earmarked purchasing power so that they joined higher-income people in having access to the best medical services.

### Affordability and Need

A phased, income-related credit would require society to determine at what income levels the credit should phase down and by how much. The determination would depend on how much assistance people needed to buy insurance.

No exact definition of *need* exists. No equation can unequivocally tell us how much individuals at different levels should pay for health insurance and how much should be offset by a credit. Such a judgment is ultimately a political one: Whom are taxpayers willing to subsidize and for how much? (Any form of subsidy, including single-payer national health insurance programs, poses the same question.)

But empirical data can guide the political question. Table 2 shows the proportion of people younger than sixty-five at each income level who are privately insured or provided with insurance by their employer. (The remainder of the population at each income level is either uninsured or receiving Medicaid or some other type of public coverage.) More than half the families with incomes at 125–150 percent of the poverty line obtain such coverage, and the proportion covered rises further as income rises. Above about 300 percent of the federal poverty line (FPL), more than 80 percent of families obtain private coverage even though the value of the exclusion is still modest. At still higher income levels and generous tax subsidies, more than 90 percent of people obtain coverage, but most of these would probably do so even if the subsidy were much less.

Society might determine that with an income level greater than 300 percent of the FPL, most people could obtain private coverage on their own—either by paying for it directly or more commonly by taking a job that provided part of the compensation in the form of tax-shielded

### TABLE 2

PRIVATE OR EMPLOYMENT-BASED HEALTH INSURANCE,
AT AGES 0–64, BY INCOME AS PERCENTAGE OF FEDERAL POVERTY LINE, 1999
(N=115,474)

| Family Income (% of Poverty line) | Percent with Some Private or Employment-Based Health Insurance |
|---|---|
| Less than 100 | 26.3 |
| 100– 124 | 45.7 |
| 125–149 | 51.8 |
| 150–174 | 58.0 |
| 175–199 | 66.2 |
| 200–249 | 73.2 |
| 250–299 | 80.1 |
| 300–399 | 85.8 |
| 400–499 | 89.1 |
| 500 and greater | 92.4 |
| Total | 74.2 |

NOTE:   The table uses post-1996 CPS health insurance variables and appropriate CPS March Supplement weights to reflect national population. Data set is CPS March Supplement for 2000, reflecting coverage in 1999. Any private or employment-based health insurance is defined as employment-based or individually purchased coverage, as a policyholder or a dependent, and includes CHAMPUS, CHAMPVA, VA, and military health care.

insurance premiums rather than higher money wages. Such an estimate of affordability is only approximate since the price of insurance also varies across people—by age, risk, geography, and size of employment group. After contemplating more refined versions of the data presented, policymakers could decide necessary additional subsidies. No matter what they decided about income levels, they should remain concerned about tax inequity within income categories between those who did and those who did not benefit from the exclusion.

Would reducing credits as incomes rose adversely affect work effort to a significant degree? The implicit "tax" in the scheme that we propose later is relatively modest. If nothing else changed, some type of compromise between good health policy and good labor market policy would be inevitable. However, the introduction of credits as part of a long-overdue comprehensive tax reform might entail less conflict. Most important, work incentives depend on how the total of all tax and subsidy provisions vary with earned income, not just on what happens to health insurance.

Specifically, one could accommodate a set of insurance credits that declined fairly steeply with income if other tax rates rose fairly slowly with income. It is the overall progressivity of the tax-and-transfer system that matters for work effort and equity, after all. If the income tax schedule were made nominally less progressive over the relevant range (still allowing for large transfers to the low-income, as even flat taxes do) but health insurance credits were phased out as incomes rose, the resulting outcome could be satisfactory. People would still argue about how progressive the total system should be—how they felt about the trade-off between work disincentives and redistribution—but there should be no need for health policy alone to shoulder the burden of deciding this balance.

# 7

# Technical Design Issues

Basically our proposal would institute a program of income-related universal (that is, not limited to certain subpopulations) credits toward the purchase of qualified health insurance. Some technical issues need to be solved along the way toward specifying how a credits plan would work.

## Cash Flow

One technical issue is how the credit would work for people who needed contemporaneous assistance to buy insurance. The issue is important but not complex. People might switch from jobs that carried employment-based insurance to those that did not. If individuals bought their own insurance in the individual market, the anticipated credit could be assigned to the insurer (and thus reduce problems of cash flow for the buyer). As suggested by our earlier discussion, if a person accepted a job that carried group insurance, the net credit could be paid directly to workers (in the form of lower tax withholding) who bought such insurance by sacrificing wages.

## Adjustment for Risk

Variation in the risk of expense is much more complex and much more difficult to deal with. Resolving the issue would require compromises.

The nongroup insurance market generally charges premiums that vary with some, though not all, indicators of risk, that is, predicted or expected total medical expenses. Research shows that although nongroup (also called *individual*) premiums increase with risk, they do so much less than proportionately (Pauly and Herring 1999). Although high risks pay more than low risks in the individual market, they pay less than their estimated average benefits, with resulting substantial transfers from low to high risks. Guaranteed renewability probably accounts in part for this pattern; the feature was common in nongroup policies even before the HIPAA mandate for all such coverage.

Given the substantial internal risk pooling, should a credit be adjusted for risk? Should a credit be larger for those who pay more for a given policy; if so, how much larger? Should a credit vary with age as premiums vary with age? As the answer is sometimes affirmative, we would need to address the administrative issue of how to produce the desired variation. In any case, getting risk adjustment right is more important at low- to moderate-income levels than at higher ones. Those with lower income have less margin to pay for insurance, whether they are high risks facing potentially high premiums or low risks facing seemingly overpriced premiums. Although credits might ideally vary with risk, substantial administrative costs might limit adjustments to those based on income and other obvious characteristics.

Varying credits proportionately with every risk factor might not be necessary. For instance, age might not be a factor requiring an adjuster. Older people would be more likely to buy coverage than younger, other things being equal. If people knew that their premiums would increase over time, they would budget ahead. Moreover, although older people generally have higher medical costs than younger people, they have lower average costs for other things, such as child care expenses. It is far from obvious why one kind of expense should be pooled and not the other.

Moreover, efforts to develop workable adjusters for all determinants of risk have not yet proved successful. Even if they were developed, they would be administratively complex and would raise concerns about privacy because they would require releasing data about an individual's information to the government to calculate the credit.

The system of credits may need to settle for imperfect adjusters. One common response to the question of risk adjustment is not to adjust the credit, but to regulate the premium. In particular even some advocates of the tax credit approach often assume that premiums should be community-rated: every insured person would be charged the same premium for coverage regardless of health status or risk (though perhaps with an adjustment for age).

Community rating, however, is often not as good as it sounds. It requires government regulation to ensure that insurance firms do not vary from the stated community rate, as has happened in some states and in the early days of the federal health maintenance organization act. If implemented, moreover, community rating could be counterproductive. Without a mandate or a credit equal to the premium, community rating would drive younger, lower-risk people from the insurance market. Even with a mandate or credit, some incentives would remain for insurers to develop ways to avoid enrolling higher-risk members. Regulatory interference would increase. Community rating might also drive insurers specializing in coverage desired by higher risks out of the market. On balance, therefore, community rating could reduce (or at best not increase) the number of people with insurance.

One simple strategy to deal with risk variation would be to adjust the credit not only for income but also for the amount of premium paid (with an overall cap), as discussed. For instance, the credit might be made a fixed proportion of the premium, perhaps with an upper limit. But such an approach raises other issues.

Proportional credits would have the effect of giving larger credits to those who paid higher premiums because they were higher risks. The credits would have the unfortunate side effect of also giving larger credits to people who paid high premiums because they were unwilling to shop for low premiums or were eager to buy lavish coverage. Moreover, if guaranteed renewability were present, premiums would not be systematically higher for those with below-average health status within any rating group; the primary effect of proportional credits would then be to encourage the purchase of more generous coverage.

The trade-offs are important. Intended to help the few who needed greater help, proportional credit would also provide disincentives to be efficient to many who had less need. Also, simply as a matter of arithmetic, using the same total amount of subsidy dollars to offer a larger per person subsidy to high-risk people would mean that fewer people would be helped than if the same funds were used for lower per person subsidies for lower risks.

For example, as shown in table 3, Pauly and Herring (2001) estimate that a 50 percent credit would reduce the number of uninsured by 30.3 percent, whereas the credit, if used as a fixed-dollar incentive, would produce a 53 percent reduction. (The estimate of difference is sensitive to the modeling assumptions, but the difference narrows sharply as the credit rises; for a two-thirds credit, the reduction in the uninsured would be 52 and 59 percent, respectively.)

Whether the credit would be fixed dollar or proportional should be less significant than the fact that either type of credit could significantly reduce the number of uninsured. It is not clear which policy would have the larger aggregate impact on health since the greater number of low risks might suffer as much in the aggregate from forgoing care when needed as the smaller number of high risks. The trade-off would depend on the relative numbers of people who could be helped as well as on social

**TABLE 3**

EFFECT OF TAX CREDITS ON THE UNINSURED, COMPREHENSIVE
INDIVIDUAL INSURANCE PLAN WITH 30 PERCENT LOADING
(percent reduction in uninsured)

| Amount of Credit (%) | Proportional Credit | Equivalent Cost (per person credit) |
|---|---|---|
| 25 | 12.0 | 27.6 |
| 33 | 17.0 | 36.2 |
| 50 | 30.3 | 53.0 |
| 66 | 51.9 | 59.0 |

NOTE: The table uses originally uninsured expense distribution and assumes costly though free care; the average premium for self-only coverage is assumed to be $1,671 (in 1996). See Pauly and Herring 2001 for details and other estimates.

perception of their relative need. We do not know enough about social preferences to make a recommendation.

Other refinements and trade-offs would be possible. As discussed, to mitigate the incentive that a proportional credit would create to purchase more expensive insurance and to be less aggressive in shopping, one could impose an overall cap on the amount of the credit. With either a fixed or proportional credit, a cap would pose a risk that some high-risk individuals would have premiums above the cap. There is no need to provide special treatment for high-risk people who can afford the higher premiums. Ultimately the policy should be based not on the assumption that every high-risk person would pay more for coverage, but rather on fail-safe provisions to protect against situations in which a high-risk individual faces exorbitant premiums.

Current federal policy in HIPAA requiring guaranteed renewability in the individual market should remain in place. We would need to see how the anticipated inflow of good risks affected the individual market before deciding to adjust regulation. If states did choose to alter how they regulated premiums, they should be required to show that any new policies would not increase the number of uninsured. However, alternatives to rate regulation can help high risks.

One such mechanism is the use of high-risk pools, now existing in most states: the person faced with high premiums for new insurance because he is an unusually high risk can find an additional subsidy by buying insurance from a high-risk pool. Typically the premium in a high-risk pool is about 150 percent of the standard premium; setting the threshold lower would run the risk of drawing a large proportion of the insured into the pool. Alternatively people could qualify for a higher credit (subsidy) paid directly to them by presenting proof that they were being charged high-risk premiums by a number of competing insurers.

A key empirical question here is how much actual premium variation is due to insurer adjustment for risk and how much is due to variation in prices and costs not related to risk. We want consumers to bear the cost of higher prices unrelated to risk so that they will be efficient shoppers. Yet if the chosen public policy decided that some protection against higher premiums were needed, the credit could be defined as a moderate proportion of the excess of the premium actually paid over the standard or average premium in a corridor until risk pool eligibility were triggered.

Such a scheme might work like this: the plan might offer individuals of a given observable set of characteristics (income, etc.) a credit of $1,500. For those who paid a premium above that amount, the credit might cover 50 percent of the additional premium up to premiums greater than 150 percent of the standard. For people quoted premiums in excess of 150 percent, a subsidized high-risk pool would be used. Those design parameters could be adjusted as experience dictated. At first a relatively larger number of people might exist in the above-average premium corridor, but if guaranteed renewability worked, that number (and the number in the high-risk pool) should shrink dramatically over time.

### Qualified Coverage

The other complex technical issue concerns the specification of a qualified policy. Here is another of the ubiquitous iron triangles of medical care finance. Public policy seems to have three objectives: getting the uninsured covered, protecting the taxpayer against uncontrolled spending on credits, and ensuring that those who are covered buy generous coverage. However, we can improve any two only by worsening the third. For example, if we offered modest credits that might be used only to buy a comprehensively generous policy, many would remain uninsured because they would not be willing or able to pay their share of the premium.

Several estimates have been made of the effects of credits in the $800–1,000 per individual range; the estimates conclude that the reduction in the number of uninsured would be small (Gruber and Levitt 2000; Shiels, Hogan, and Haught 1999) without a mandate. These estimates generally assume that the person must buy a fairly expensive policy to use the credit at all and naturally conclude that many uninsured would not pay enough additional out of their own incomes to obtain such a policy.

Alternatively, virtually universal acceptance of a modest credit would result if it could be used for any policy and were not limited to a comprehensive policy (Pauly and Herring 2001). Finally, everyone could be enrolled in a policy that covered a wide range of services with low-cost sharing and little managed care interference, but the credits needed to do so would have a high aggregate budget cost.

How might one specify the policy that would qualify for the credit? At one extreme medical experts could design what the basic benefit package would cover, and the government could adopt the design as the required minimum policy. The result would almost surely be fairly comprehensive coverage at high premiums. Unless the credit covered almost all that high premium, many people would reject the credit—and coverage—entirely since they would be unwilling to pay their share of the premium.

At the other extreme the same dollar credit could be permitted to be used for any health coverage (insurance or the direct provision of services through a managed care plan) permitted under state law, without federal requirements for coverage of specific services or limits on copayments, deductibles, or limits. Plans could be offered to provide at least some coverage for the amount of the credit.

We tend to favor the second approach for several reasons. Americans are best capable of judging what coverage is best for them. Some may want high deductibles and coinsurance in exchange for fewer restrictions on obtaining care; others may be willing to accept more restrictions to obtain a lower premium. There must be protection to ensure that the coverage is not a subterfuge for converting the credit into cash. But the federal government should not attempt to define qualified coverage. The decision should be left to the states; if coverage could be bought in a state, the credit could be used for it. States might take different regulatory approaches.

Some policy analysts or advocates might attempt to define a basic policy. The attempt would inevitably lead to regulation, rigidities, political pressure by providers and disease groups to be included, and thus the politicization of health care. The process would remove diversity and flexibility in both the insurance and the health care delivery market. Defining a policy in any but the broadest terms is an illusory process. Trying to specify the precise factors of when care should be covered would result in government control and uniformity when freedom and flexibility were needed. Accordingly states would be advised to define the policy in the broadest terms, for instance, like the definition of the services that a plan must cover to participate in the Federal Employees Health Benefits Plan (essentially, hospital and medical services, drugs, and medical supplies). But each state would determine the definition of services.

With a proportional credit a state could increase the amount of federal funds drawn into the state by imposing extensive requirements on plans. However, even with a proportional credit, the consumer would pay some of the premium (the percentage depending on income) and might therefore resist state regulations that increased the cost of coverage by more than the expected additional value. In addition the credit could be subject to an overall cap.

Finally, the best should not be made the enemy of the good. The primary objective should be some coverage for those who had none. Whether that coverage was considered ideal by some definition should be of less immediate concern. The more we restricted the qualified policy, the more we would induce people to reject the credit entirely—exactly the opposite of our primary policy goal.

The acceptance rate of a policy with a premium close to the value of the credit should be large. The smaller the credit, the less comprehensive the policy would be. Although some assume that a policy is a decent one only if it covers all expenses, the purpose of insurance is actually to protect against large unbudgetable expenses by spreading the risk. A credit for the nonpoor that would permit the purchase of such a policy would restore perspective to insurance (at least for those using the credit). The change would also contain increases in health care costs and help restore the traditional doctor-patient relationship. The common but erroneous assumption that insurance must cover every transaction (and therefore potentially control every transaction) has been harmful in that respect.

The main objection to offering credits that could be used for partial individual coverage is that the insurer's administrative cost for a small policy per dollar of benefits paid might be high. The cost might exceed the cost for a government-run limited safety-net program (Blumberg 1999). The cost would potentially be a problem if the credit were quite small, but we have in mind fairly substantial credits (on the order of about 50 percent of the premium for a comprehensive policy). Moreover, if a frugal but decent public program could offer better value than private insurance, it could be converted into explicit insurance and made one of the options for people eligible for the credit.

The extent to which a credit program would increase insurance coverage could be determined only by observing how an actual program worked and then evaluating its performance. Faced with a huge potential market of people who preferred modestly priced insurance, insurers might be creative in developing a policy that limited the terms of coverage to what people could afford. Whether that policy should take the form of catastrophic coverage, medical savings accounts, rigorous managed care, integrated provider systems, or some other method yet to be devised is a question that perplexes politicians but that consumers armed with credits can answer best.

# 8

# A Tax-Credit Plan

Designing a plan of tax credits to cover the uninsured would necessarily be a political task since it would depend on the trade-offs that citizens (or their elected representatives) would be willing to make among the various objectives, including distributional ones. Here we sketch out a plan with the features already discussed as desirable. The quantitative indicators would be subject, however, to fine tuning as political preferences and new empirical information dictated.

The most important quantitative features of the kind of tax-credit plan that we propose are the size and the form of the subsidy to be offered at various income levels. Table 4 shows subsidy rates for proportional-credit and fixed-dollar contributions (benchmarked at the average proportional subsidy) for a five-step income-conditioned credit plan.

A comprehensive policy could be purchased at a premium of $2,400 for an individual and $6,000 for family. Those with incomes below the poverty line would receive free insurance, and those with incomes up to 200 percent of poverty would pay only $50 per month for individual coverage or $125 per month for family coverage. Those families would generally pay less than 10 percent of their income for health insurance.

In all cases those numbers represent the credit net of the value of any exclusion. Those with lower incomes would almost surely claim a credit,

## TABLE 4
### PROPOSED INSURANCE CREDIT AMOUNTS

| Income as Percent of Federal Poverty Line | Fixed-Dollar Credit, Family | Fixed-Dollar Credit, Self | Proportional Credit (%) |
|---|---|---|---|
| Less than 100 | $6,000 | $2,400 | 100 |
| 100–200 | $4,500 | $1,800 | 75 |
| 200–300 | $3,000 | $1,200 | 50 |
| 300–400 | $1,800 | $720 | 30 |
| Greater than 400 | $1,200 | $480 | 20 |

but the great majority of those in higher-income categories would probably prefer to retain the exclusion or (in the case of self-employed) a tax deduction to using the credit.

The credit could be used on any state-licensed or self-insured plan of an employer that covered medical and surgical expenses. Those meeting the income eligibility for a credit would automatically be enrolled in a low-cost insurance plan with a premium equal to the credit. As discussed in our earlier work, a state would designate the fallback insurer. That could be a contracted private insurer, a program administered by the state (and part of its Medicaid or Children's Health Insurance Program, CHIP), or a new public insurance plan. Offering a politically selected insurer option might be a benchmark for private plans and an option that some citizens might prefer to a private plan. The further alternative of Medicaid and free care would remain. Beyond state approval and a broad definition of coverage, few restrictions would be placed on the kinds of policies that would qualify for the credit.

The credit should be refundable, income related, and universal. Political compromise, however, may be found in limiting the credit to those who pay income or payroll taxes, with Medicaid offered to all other low-income persons. As to the choice between flat and proportional credits, we think that one could start with either one but be prepared to move to the other.

# 9

# Objections and Problems

Two practical concerns exist about the kind of scheme that we propose; they relate to transition issues and to the fear of substitution. Some people fear that high-risk workers and dependents might be harmed if the current subsidy biased toward employment group coverage were made more neutral. Others worry that offering a credit would shrink the sizable sums (in the form of premiums and wage reductions) that people currently pay toward their own insurance and that the tax-financed credit would crowd out private payments.

Tax-credit schemes are not intended to destroy employment-based group insurance. The insurance now obtained in connection with a job enjoys a unique subsidy. As a result of the bias, some people have employment-related coverage even though they find it irritating and unresponsive. Our goal, however, is not to kill employer coverage, but rather to have it compete on a level footing with other ways of choosing and administering insurance. Employees almost surely would prefer a carefully managed, sensitive, efficiently administered large-employer group plan to any alternative plan. Any employer convinced of its value in organizing coverage could require as a condition of employment that workers join the firm's plan (and employees could use their credit as their contribution to the plan). Under our scheme workers could use their credits to obtain group coverage regardless of how a group is organized or who sponsors the group. The good groups would survive—and any employer group in today's competitive labor market must be good.

Most worrisome to skeptics of tax credits is the fear that even if a current employment-based group plan were better for many of a firm's workers, the plan might not be better for everyone. Credits might somehow allow those workers to break out of the group and thus unravel the entire arrangement.

No one can offer ironclad guarantees, but such danger is minimal. Nongroup insurance would not likely be advantageous even for the younger, lower-risk workers, the usual suspect escapees. Suppose that a twenty-six-year-old worked for a firm with workers of varying ages that contributed an average of $3,500 per worker toward health insurance. Armed with a tax credit at least as large as the current tax subsidy, would that younger worker alone be better off entering the nongroup market? The answer would surely be negative.

Most obvious, any insurance policy would be more costly in a nongroup setting. A young worker who wanted to be skimmed therefore would need enough back from dropping out of the pool to offset these higher costs. The young worker who contemplated dropping employment group coverage would not automatically (or even probably) get $3,500 more in money wages from a comparable job in a firm that did not offer insurance.

Indeed, since wages increase with age (a proxy for experience or seniority), even a firm with only young workers would have no advantage over the firm with a heterogeneous work force. (Research shows that firms offering health insurance reduce the size of the "seniority increments" to workers compared with what happens to otherwise similar workers who do not receive health insurance; see Sheiner 1994 and Pauly and Herring 1999.) The wage offset in the all–twenty-six-year-olds firm would equal the small cost of group coverage for such workers—but the wage reduction for the young workers in the heterogeneous firm should be no larger. Each worker's pay would be reduced by the expected cost of coverage for his age group, with younger workers giving up less because on average they cost less. If a worker received approximately what the employer spent for coverage for people of his age, he would not have nearly enough to buy individual coverage, even at premiums adjusted for age, because of the substantially higher administrative cost that such premiums must cover. The argument would also apply to employer decisions.

Firms that do not offer insurance often pay lower money wages (and do not attract workers of comparable skill). If a firm dropped coverage, it would not find it necessary to provide $3,500 more in compensation to continue to attract some twenty-six-year-olds. With only a modest amount of extra wages, dropping out of a large group and using one's credit in the more expensive nongroup market might not look like a better deal to young employees than staying with the group as long as the group offered decent insurance.

If a firm were relatively small and the employer did not make a wise choice about coverage, all employees, young and old, might prefer alternative insurance arrangements. Small, poorly administered groups would be vulnerable to defection (as they should); some workers (young or not) might really not value health insurance and might prefer even a small amount of extra income. However, keeping the group intact would offer such substantial administrative advantages that sensible employers interested in maintaining a role with insurance would not want to let many such workers escape into the world of individual insurance. If the efficiency of providing individual insurance improved substantially, workers, young or old, might drop out of the group.

Neutral tax credits would affect few efficient group insurance-purchasing arrangements. Most workers and employers would stay put. The phase-in of credits should be monitored to flag any large-scale defections. But a fear of a small problem for a few persons could not justify rejecting the substantial benefit of tax-credit plans for other people who did not have the opportunity to obtain employment-based group coverage.

Another aspect of our plan might concern practical people: the likelihood that substantial portions of the tax-credit funds would replace current payments for insurance from the insured. Academics can say that credits to people who already bought insurance without a subsidy or with a much smaller subsidy are only transfers, but real politicians know that government money is not free to the government; a credit is a transfer of tax revenue from the government to the individual. Once returned to taxpayers, politicians would have difficulty reclaiming it for taxes.

A principled philosophic stance on tax equity means that the transfer should not be viewed as a problem. The best way to deal with the practicalities of tax cuts (or tax increases) is to phase them in—gradually according to an agreed plan tied to growth in the overall economy and the level of tax collection from other instruments.

Making credits most generous for the low-income with subsequent phase-down for rising income would offer advantages of equity and efficiency. But that determination would provide an implicit tax on higher money income, which would add to the marginal tax inherent in the progressive tax structure and to the phase-out of the earned income tax credit. Our sample plan would involve an additional marginal tax of only 10 percent. The tax rate could be limited either by cutting the size of the credit offered to the low-income or by extending the range of incomes for which the credit was offered. We would generally prefer the latter course, although some compromises might be possible. Moreover, if the entire tax structure were overhauled, reducing the rates in the lower brackets to offset the health credits might improve a system of health insurance credits.

# 10

# Conclusion

About 40 million Americans have no health insurance. The current economic downturn is likely to increase the number of uninsured significantly. The fact that health insurance is already subsidized for those with coverage through their employer—resulting in a higher tax subsidy for those with higher incomes and those with more expensive insurance—is increasingly being understood. That recognition may help create the political will to address the crisis of the uninsured.

The conditions are in place, moreover, to do so properly. Efforts to reform the entire health care system in one comprehensive scheme died along with the health care bill of the Clinton administration. So too did the idea of imposing mandates on employers to provide insurance or on individuals to buy it. The public and politicians generally agree that reform can only be incremental. And support is increasing, across party lines, for a tax credit or voucher to assist the uninsured in buying insurance.

Since taxpayers are probably not willing to finance all care for all people, it becomes necessary for society to determine whom it wishes to subsidize, how much subsidy it wishes to provide, and what mechanisms should be used to deliver it. Those questions derive from one that is even more fundamental: what is the purpose of the subsidy? Is it to provide tax equity in relation to those who have employer-provided insurance? Is it to provide basic coverage (that is, coverage against the largest expenses) for everyone? Or is it to provide coverage for those who present a higher health risk and thus have higher premiums? In short, how should the necessarily finite pot of money available for the subsidy be allocated, and what would it be intended to purchase?

Those questions have no technically exact answers. They are necessarily and appropriately political. The concerns documented here should help society value various options and set the parameters for fashioning a credit/voucher program.

The first question is what population the credit should target. Should the credit/voucher be available as an alternative for those eligible for Medicaid and for those who receive the tax subsidy for employment-provided insurance? The credit should be universal—available to all people at any particular income level, with mechanisms to ensure that those also eligible for Medicaid or the exclusion for employer-provided insurance do not double dip—and it should be income related to use tax assistance for those most in need of it for insurance. A voucher or refundable tax credit would assist those whose tax obligations were less than the subsidy. The short-run political situation might call for limiting the credit to those who paid taxes (including payroll taxes), while measures were taken to expand Medicaid or a Medicaid-like program for those who did not.

The American people through Congress must determine how much assistance to provide at various income levels. We suggest as a tool in making such a decision consideration of the ability and willingness of people to purchase insurance at various income levels. Data on affordability with the percentages of people at any particular income level who obtained insurance (at current tax subsidies, which we are not proposing to reduce now) could inform the decision of where the subsidy must be focused.

The purpose of the credit is not only to assist people to obtain insurance but also to provide tax equity. Two families with the same income should not receive different subsidies simply because one already bought insurance without extra assistance and the other did not. If anything, the former should be rewarded for responsible behavior. The appropriate analysis would consider not merely how many people would be newly insured because of the subsidy but how horizontal tax equity could be enhanced. Although a credit that declined as income rose could not restore tax equity damaged by the exclusion for people at higher-income levels, the credit would enhance tax equity at lower levels. For complete reform and overall fairness, some limits on the exclusion would be helpful as well.

Any major federal subsidy program would face the possibility of federal regulation of the market in which the subsidy would be used. The subsidy for employer-provided insurance did not initially lead to federal regulation of the insurance market, perhaps because that subsidy was "merely" an exclusion from taxable income (and thus was less visible). Regulation did eventually arrive with the passage of the HIPAA law. A credit or voucher for individuals to buy insurance, however, would be a more direct and visible subsidy—one of its advantages. At the same time, that visibility of the subsidy would increase the risk of extensive regulation. If the government explicitly provided a subsidy for a stated purpose, it would be more attuned to whether the subsidy had the desired effect. The danger would be posed particularly if recipients of the credit could not obtain the insurance product that some in society had determined they should. In that event the government might find it politically easier to force the market to shape itself to the credit than to modify the subsidy. The government could regulate insurance in a way that would on paper make the credit "work" but would likely reduce access to insurance. To avoid that dynamic, the credit/voucher should be structured to reduce the inevitable temptation to regulate the insurance market.

The major question is the amount of the credit. It could be a fixed amount, one based on a rough determination of the price of insurance, how much people at a given income level should be expected to pay out of their own pocket for the insurance, and how much money would be available in the budget for the credit. A fixed credit would be administratively the simplest way to provide the assistance. It would give the same assistance to people at different risk levels. However, because insurers naturally adjust premiums for perceived risk (however imperfectly), a fixed-amount credit would mean that higher-risk individuals at the same income level would tend to have higher premiums and thus higher payments net of the fixed credit, and lower-risk individuals would face lower net premiums. Thus more low-risk people would buy insurance, while fewer higher-risk people would do so.

Instead of a fixed credit, each individual's credit could be adjusted on the basis of risk. However, satisfactory risk-adjusters have not been developed. Even if they existed, they would by definition be based on individual circumstances. The adjusters would therefore be complex for the government to administer. And they would present serious concerns about privacy; the government would have to know relevant health information about every American eligible (or indeed potentially eligible) for the credit. Even then, nothing would guarantee that insurers would rate individuals in the same way as the government adjusted the credit. That uncertainty could force government regulation of how insurers set premiums.

Synchronizing the credit with the premium could require insurance companies to use community rating of premiums. That requirement would make administration of the subsidy simpler than if the subsidy were risk adjusted. The community-rated premium for each carrier would be known, and the government could determine its subsidy without concern for individual variation. However, community rating would entail intrusive and widespread regulation to ensure compliance by insurers. And without a mandate requiring people to obtain insurance (which we assume would not be politically viable and would raise concerns about personal freedom), a community-rating system would discourage some low-risk people from buying insurance even with a credit.

Another approach would avoid government interference in rating decisions and would reduce the need to develop and apply risk-adjusters to the credit. The credit could be proportional; it could be a percentage of the premium paid (with the percentage being higher for low-income individuals and lower for high-income people). Low-risk people (at any given income level) would still pay less on an absolute basis than high-risk people, but high-risk people would have a larger credit if their premiums were higher.

But that approach cannot distinguish between lazy purchasing and excessively rich insurance packages on the one hand and high risk on the other. The higher payment by an individual in absolute terms as the premium increased would provide some brake to the process. To ensure a limit on the subsidy, however, the credit could be capped at a reasonable amount. An individual without a subsidy would fully pay any premium above that amount.

The cap would present another problem: an extremely high-risk person, no matter how careful a purchaser, could spend more than the cap. In that case other mechanisms could be introduced. The individual could be placed in a high-risk pool run by insurers in the market or if necessary by the state. Or the credit could be adjusted if the individual demonstrated that several insurers had quoted premiums above the cap.

The other major parameter would specify what the credit/voucher could be used for. Again caution would be needed so that the provision of a subsidy did not result in excessive regulation of the product. There would be a temptation to impose expensive requirements on qualified plans and to use insurance to reach other desired social goals. Prescriptive regulation and expansive standards would make the program more complex and the insurance product more expensive and would thus reduce the acceptance rate.

In particular, defining a minimum benefit package in detail should be avoided. The process would inevitably politicize health care. Any prescribed minimum benefit, while comforting on paper, could be illusory when confronted with the real world. Because of the many variables in health care delivery, the effort to enforce any attempted definition would result in rigidification and homogenization of plans and extensive regulatory efforts to enforce compliance.

The credit should be usable for any health coverage that can legally be sold in a taxpayer's state. Nothing could prevent a state from imposing mandates (except a federal preemption—which would result only in turning the regulation over to the federal government). But variation among the states would provide information on the extent to which mandates and other regulation of plans raised costs. With such comparative information, Americans could balance the value of the regulatory structure against its effect on the price and availability of insurance.

The point that we emphasize is that the credit/voucher should be introduced in a common sense way, with as much simplicity and flexibility as possible. Rather than trying to anticipate and solve every issue that may arise (which in any event is impossible and would unnecessarily complicate the plan), it should be introduced, and adjustment should be made as necessary, aimed at the particular problems identified.

# References

Altman, S. H. 1999. Overview address to the Health Sector Assembly, Park City, Utah, October 30.

Arnett, G. M., ed. 1999. *Empowering Health Care Consumers through Tax Reform.* Ann Arbor: University of Michigan Press.

Berndt, E. 2000. "The U.S. Pharmaceutical Industry: Why Significant Growth in This Time of Cost Containment?" *Health Affairs* 20 (2) (March–April): 100–114.

Blumberg, L. J. 1999. "Who Pays for Employer-Sponsored Health Care?" *Health Affairs* 18 (6) (November–December): 58–61.

Bowman, Karlyn. 1998. "Health Care Attitudes Today." American Enterprise Institute study. Accessed October 26, 2001, at www.aei.org/ps/psbowman.htm.

Butler, S. M., and E. F. Haislmaier. 1992. *A Policy Maker's Guide to the Health Care Crisis.* Heritage Foundation's Talking Points Series. Washington, D.C.: Heritage.

Calfee, J. E. 2000. *Prices, Markets, and the Pharmaceutical Revolution.* Washington, D.C.: AEI Press.

Cutler, D. M., M. McClellan, and J. Newhouse. 1998. *The Costs and Benefits of Intensive Treatment for Cardiovascular Disease.* National Bureau of Economic Research Working Paper 6514. Washington, D.C.: NBER.

Gruber, J., and J. Levitt. 2000. "Tax Subsidies for Health Insurance: Costs and Benefits." *Health Affairs* 19 (1) (January–February): 72–85.

Helms, R. B. 2001. "Positive Economics and Dismal Politics: The Role of Tax Policy in the Current Health Policy Debate." In *The Political Economy of Health Care Reforms,* edited by Huizhong Zhou, pp. 125–46. Kalamazoo, Mich.: W. E. Upjohn Institute for Employment Research.

Himmelstein, D. U., and S. Woolhandler. 1991. "Debating National Health Insurance Alternatives." *Health Affairs* 10 (2) (summer): 223–24, 227–28.

Lemieux, J., D. Kendall, and S. R. Levine. 2000. "A Progressive Path toward Universal Health Coverage." Progressive Policy Institute Policy Report, December 20.

O'Neill, J. E., and D. M. O'Neill. 1994. *The Employment and Distributional Effects of Mandated Benefits.* Washington, D.C.: AEI Press.

Pauly, M. V. 1994a. "The Clinton Plan: What Happened to the Tough Choices?" *Health Affairs* 13 (6) (spring): 147–60.

48

————. 1994b. "Universal Health Insurance in the Clinton Plan: Coverage as a Tax-Financed Public Good." *Journal of Economic Perspectives* 8 (3) (summer): 45–53.

————. 1999a. "Medical Care Costs, Benefits, and Effects: Conceptual Issues for Measuring Price Changes." In *Measuring the Prices of Medical Treatments,* edited by J. Triplett, pp. 196–219. Washington, D.C.: Brookings Institution Press.

————. 1999b. "An Efficient and Equitable Approach to Health Reform." In *Empowering Health Care Consumers through Tax Reform,* edited by G. M. Arnett, pp. 55–70. Ann Arbor: University of Michigan Press.

Pauly, M. V., P. Danzon, P. Feldstein, and J. Hoff. 1991. "A Plan for 'Responsible National Health Insurance.'" *Health Affairs* 10 (1) (spring): 5–25.

————. 1992. *Responsible National Health Insurance.* Washington, D.C.: AEI Press.

Pauly, M. V., and J. Goodman. 1995. "Credits for Health Insurance and Medical Savings Accounts in Incremental Steps toward Health Care Reform." *Health Affairs* 14 (1) (spring): 125–39.

Pauly, M. V., and B. Herring. 1999. *Pooling Health Insurance Risks.* Washington, D.C.: AEI Press.

————. 2001. "Expanding Insurance Coverage through Tax Credits: Tradeoffs and Options." *Health Affairs* 20 (1) (January–February): 1–18.

Pauly, M. V., A. Percy, and B. Herring. 1999. "Individual versus Job-Based Health Insurance: Weighing the Pros and Cons." *Health Affairs* 18 (6) (November–December): 28–44.

Sheils, J., P. Hogan, and R. Haught. 1999. "Health Insurance and Taxes: The Impact of Proposed Changes in Current Federal Policy." Paper prepared for the National Coalition on Health Care, October 18, Washington, D.C.

Sheiner, L. 1994. "Health Care Costs, Wages, and Aging: Assessing the Impact of Community Rating." Federal Reserve Board. December.

Triplett, J. E., ed. 1999. *Measuring the Prices of Medical Treatments.* Washington, D.C.: Brookings Institution Press.

U.S., Bureau of the Census. 2001. *Health Insurance Coverage: 2000.* Department of Commerce, Current Population Reports, P60-215, September.

# About the Authors

MARK V. PAULY is professor of health care systems, insurance and risk management, and public policy and management at the Wharton School, professor of economics at the School of Arts and Sciences, and Bendheim Professor, University of Pennsylvania. He is a member of the Institute of Medicine and an adjunct scholar of AEI.

Mr. Pauly was the director of research and the executive director, Leonard Davis Institute of Health Economics; a visiting research fellow, International Institute of Management; a commissioner, Physical Payment Review Commission; and professor of economics, Northwestern University. He is on numerous editorial boards and has written more than one hundred journal articles.

He is the author of *Financing Long-Term Care: What Should Be the Government's Role?* with Peter Zweifel (AEI Press, 1996), *An Analysis of Medical Savings Accounts: Do Two Wrongs Make a Right?* (AEI Press, 1994), and *Responsible National Health Insurance* with Patricia Danzon, Paul Feldstein, and Mr. Hoff (AEI Press, 1992).

JOHN S. HOFF is a health care lawyer and policy analyst in Washington, D.C. Mr. Hoff has written *Medicare Private Contracting: Paternalism or Autonomy?* (AEI Press, 1999) and is a coauthor of *Responsible National Health Insurance*.